Dr. Simeon S. Mayuga
5306 W. Irving St.
Pasco, WA 99301-3004

POEMS OF ENDEARMENT AND MORE

By
Enriqueta Cartagena Mayuga

Oct. 13, 2024

Dear Maryann —
this summates Life —
yours, mine and all.
God bless you (my 8th Book)
with prayer and devotion
E. C. Mayuga

POEMS OF ENDEARMENT AND MORE
Copyright © 2022 by Enriqueta Cartagena Mayuga

All rights reserved. No part of this publication may be reproduced, distributed, or transmitted in any form or by any means, including photocopying, recording, or other electronic or mechanical methods, without the prior written permission of the publisher, except in the case brief quotations embodied in critical reviews and other noncommercial uses permitted by copyright law.

ISBN: (Paperback)   978-1-63945-442-6
       (Hardback)   978-1-63945-444-0
       (Ebook)   978-1-63945-443-3

The views expressed in this book are solely those of the author and do not necessarily reflect the views of the publisher, and the publisher hereby disclaims any responsibility for them.

Writers' Branding
1800-608-6550
www.writersbranding.com
orders@writersbranding.com

Contents

About the Author vii
Dedication ix
Introduction xi
Preface...xiii
Acknowledgements..xv

Chapter I
Romance

The Gilded Life of My Imaginings 2
Endless Love 3
Isabella... 4
By the Power of Love 6
The Final Romance 8
New Romance, Old Romance 9
My Soul's Sustenance 11

Chapter II
Endurance and Attrition

I Know My Place 14
A Straggler for Life..16
Why? How?..17
Neverland..19
Thoughts...20
But It Hurts As Much 21
Closure 23

Chapter III
Bonding

He Will Be Back - My Son.................................26
He at 80..27

My Papa Would Be Mighty Proud 28
The Awaited 29
Alma 31
My Papa's Canoe and Me 33
Latino Is In 34
I Chose America 36
Our Son Is Back - It Is Harvest Time 38

Chapter IV
Wisdom and Transition

Life's Performance 42
I Got In (A Case for Affirmative Action) 44
Forgiving the Enemy 46
America Is Not for All 47
A Transplant 48
Mea Culp - from an immigrant's child 50
No Such Thing as Charred Hope 53
From Both Sides Now 54
Sunshine is my Ally 56

Chapter V
Wonderment and Hope

Let the Day Begin: Life's Amalgam 60
Born Free 62
Not the Meekest Lamb 63
Am Ready for the Bloom 64
Never Too Late for a New Bud 65
Always the Spirit Flows 66
Spring, Autumn, Sunset 68
This Is My Moment 70
Life Is Beautiful 72

About the Author

Enriqueta Cartagena Mayuga was born in the Philippines on December 18, 1937. She obtained her medical degree from the University of Santo Tomas. Her residency and fellowship training were at Harlem Hospital, Rochester General Hospital, and at the University of Texas in San Antonio. She is a diplomate in Obstetrics/Gynecology and has been in solo private practice for over 54 years until she retired in December 2021.

Her parents, Dr. Joaquin Cartagena, a pioneering physician, and Rosario Vendivil, a pharmacist and leading educator, were political and public figures. She is the youngest of five siblings and has been married to Simeon Mayuga for 60 years and has two children and five grandchildren.

Having lived through the remnants of the Second World War, some of the episodes in her first book, Immigrant at Peace – A Woman Physician Reflects, published in 1997, bear her impressions and experiences.

She has published a total of six books of which three were pure poetry. She has won awards in various literary competitions and has appeared in various Barnes & Noble venues – also including appearances at the Los Angeles book fair and the Filipino Consulate in Los Angeles and New York. She has been an active community leader serving for the last 40 years in various organizations and served as a Board of Trustee for 10 years in Columbia Basin College

This anthology of poems was chosen from at least four of the six books written. In preparing this anthology, she wants the readers to reflect on the over 84 years of her odyssey as one who came initially to be a medical trainee and hesitantly decided to pursue writing as more than an outlet, only to find a new passion.

Other books published and written are:

1. Immigrant at Peace - 1997
2. Spring, Autumn, Sunset - 2000
3. Outspoken and Mute: American Life - 2005
4. Splintered Dreams, Blades of Truth, Shafts of Sunlight - 2009
5. Landscape of a Challenged Life - 2012
6. Speckled Prism - 2016

Books 4-6 can be ordered at Barnes & Noble and books 1-3 can be ordered by calling 509-438-6787.

Dedication

Dedicated to my grandchildren:

Sofia, Isabella, and Aidan Morrison
&
Pilar and Joaquin Mayuga

Because of them, I will always reach for the stars.

Introduction

By Dr. B. Gloria Guzman Johannessen

In ***Poems of Endearment and More*** Enriqueta Mayuga reveals a life that in its beginning was tainted by the horror of war and Japanese oppression followed by the subsequent American colonization. Later, as an American immigrant and professional, her experiences were often contaminated by discriminatory practices with the effect of making her feel "culturally discounted". While these circumstances would have negatively affected any individual, her determination to succeed enabled her to form a beautiful family, establish a successful career as a medical doctor, and become a prolific writer. She molded her world with the spirit of giving, forgiving, love, and perseverance, evident in her writings. In her latest publication, "Poems of Endearment and More", she relates many of her life experiences, but most significantly, this poetry book is a testimony of her love, not only for those who surround her, but also for country, profession and for those with whom she comes in contact.

This poetry book will enthrall the readers to look at their world in its various structures and contradictions. Each one of its five chapters is dedicated to a particular theme: Love, passion, struggle, forgiveness, or redemption as formulas for the realization of the self. The poems weave and maintain the strength and momentum of themes evoking the significance of God, country, family, work, and common relationships. Themes that encourage personal reflection on the beauty of life when it is guided by faith, love, and perseverance. While each chapter introduces particular ideas and arguments, some are intertwined with other themes which serve to strengthen or highlight the complexity of human experience.

This artfully constructed poetry book will move the readers toward an intellectual and emotional voyage of life experiences evidenced by the poetic thought of E. Mayuga's whose poems are based on her personal life trajectory based on love, acceptance, and forgiveness.

Poems of Endearment and More is a book for everyone, especially for whose interests go beyond the appreciation of delightful poetry and wish to examine life from the lenses of faith, love, and redemption. It is a must read for women, and in particular minority women.

Dr. B. Gloria Guzman Johannessen

Professor Emeritus from California State University Pomona.

Preface

Last year, with the world immersed with Covid and its repercussions – not knowing when the pandemic will end, I turned my attention to reviewing books. I began with the books I have authored– all six of them composed of poetry, prose and short stories. As I read them, copious tears started trickling down my once winsome face – now weathered by time and attrition. It seems like it was only yesterday - I felt the same pain, the same pangs - shedding the same tears.

In 1963, I came as a medical trainee, set for five years of specialty training. As soon as I set foot in the hospital and interacted with the hospital authorities, I knew that I would have to work and study hard, consoled by the thought that I would return to my native Philippines one day. In 1997, at the age of 60, after 34 years in America, including 17 years of private medical practice, I was concerned that my progenies would not understand my severe loneliness and feelings of alienation in this favored and much heralded land of promise. Writing my first book became a priority. My soul was still in turmoil; I felt this book would bring peace and solace for myself along with the hope that my children will somehow leaf through each page and understand my feelings of being marginalized in a society that was not prepared for my time.

After my first book, which was highlighted by Barnes & Noble, I found myself writing again every 2-3 years. This served as a catharsis to all my despair, impatience, and frustration. Upon reviewing my last 3 books, I noted how gentle and conciliatory my language was compared to my earlier writings. In this 7th book, an anthology, I decided to have 5 chapters which map my morphing into what I am today.

At the age of 84, I am still a fighter- but not as gutsy as in my prime. I have not retreated from my condemnation of man's callousness and injustice, but now realize that we human beings live in our own time and space, and we can only get better. I now understand that racism and discrimination are not the sole monopoly of America. As I look back, I see the instances I interpreted as discrimination could also be interpreted as cronysim and favoritism. At times, it is difficult for me to know where one begins and where the other ends. Each moment, each day, augers a new beginning for all of us - giving time for self renewal with its unending epiphanies.

This book is made for the readers' introspection, to be aware that we all live in an imperfect world. Even a determined altruistic person like me has to change and look at life's woes in a much broader fashion - less vitriolic, more tender, and more forgiving. The poems within each chapter reflect this transformation.

Enriqueta Cartagena Mayuga

Acknowledgements

I could not have completed this book without the guidance of the editor and learned friends. My gratitude is immeasurable. I appreciate their expertise and support, especially from the following:

My precious friend and longtime mentor, Tanya Sorenson Becker Ed.D., has been with me the last 25 years. She has enhanced my life as a critic, edited most of my books, and made so much impact in my literary and intellectual life. Without her, I do not believe I would have
reached this point.

My dear friend, Dr. B. Gloria Guzman Johannessen, Professor Emeritus from California State University Pomona, for her Introduction and counsel.

Sallie Fisher, English Professor at Columbia Basin College, for advising me.

Dawn Alford and Roxanne Wokanjance, for their input and support.

Cherry Safford, my long time surrogate niece, for patiently redoing the transcription from the six prior books.

Agnes Saquilayan and Myla Din, who have always been there for me, in all aspects.

I do not think I could have navigated through this process without the utmost dedication from my oldest grandchild, Sofia Morrison.

I thank my supportive family including my children Enrico and Lorena, and my loving husband, Simeon.

Thank you to the talented artist, Melissa Gloria, for providing the personalized, inventive, and outstanding sketches for the chapter pages.

Finally, Megan Grey, the primary mover and the go to person in all the phases of this publication. She has gone over and beyond what is required in order to get this book ready for publication. I am eternally grateful.

Chapter I
Romance

The Gilded Life of My Imaginings

I cannot give you my tomorrow,
    If so — my today would be for naught,
I cannot strum yesterday's guitar
    — if so, my heart would break,
So much vested with your mirage
    You were the centerfold of my life
    — my own sunlight I missed,
        in my solitary stonewalled shell.

Flecks of radiance now pass
    Through the inner atrium of my heart
    — and the singing stars twinkle in joy,
    their victorious cry —
        becomes the automatic awakenings
        of my stupor.

Dark curtains once more re-open
    my illuminated world,
Shafts of moonlight in angelic bursts
    permeating my seamless earthly wings,
I am at last free
    Reveling in my resurgent dreams
        to the beckoning of my trusted God
        to the gilded life of my imaginings.

Endless Love

Conspire with me —
    these myriad waves of ecstasy,
        Unrehashed, unrehearsed,
  no guilt, no second thoughts
      — no iota of doubt.
Bathe me in the music of love,
    your angelic bride,
Partake with me in this feast of life,
    awash in this yearning,
        this golden joy —
No longer a tortured soul,
    I float and glide
        in infinity
Infused with love's acclaim.

My night teems with effusive stars
    — effacing vestigial tales
        of woes and wants,
        of scorns and denials
            — rejections and disgrace,
With dignity, I lay my case
    bring you this burning joy,
        buried in this ecstasy:
            my endless toil, this fairy tale.

Isabella

You are what I am not —
    You are what I will never be,
You, the oasis in my barren life,
    You, the fire of my flaming flesh,
You are the tears I will forever shed,
You are the passion I never had,
    The penumbra of my soul —
The surviving rose of my twilight years,
    The calm composure of the spring —
The ultimate contentment — my everything.

I adore you for just being you—
    Your soul unblemished by age and time,
Untraveled trails and tenuous heights —
You trek, undaunted by the task,
    In the face of unspeakable woes,
    — past the howling, cruel foe.
You are the rainbow we all can see,
    — but longingly could never touch,
You are the heaven of my lofty quest,
    The ultimate end of my sensual nest.

You are the wave which buoyed me up —
You nurtured me through my listless flights,
Amidst the dust and forsaken weeds —
    In time you save my soul, indeed,
Past the pains of atrocious nights —
    The gem in you gave God delight,
The seeds you've sown bore redeeming fruits —
    nourishing me with lovely thoughts,
Awakening me — my life of flaws,
    From wobbly sails, my disabled bow.

Because of you, I have no night,
      Cold winter comes as pure delight,
The clouds and the rain appear to be,
      — nothing more but eternity,
Lightning comes as a sparkling glow —
Thunder sounds like a roaring flow,
      brooking no ill to lives below —
Animating the embittered souls,
Wounded pride and outrage killed,
      By your limpid grace and soul fulfilled.

If my life were to end this very day —
      I will cling to your peace and endearing ways,
I would forever breathe with beaming joy
      — knowing that you are heaven's ploy.
I would be ready to face my God —
For you soothe my sores and errors mad,
      — past the judgment I should have had,
      — had you not come into my life,
Past my sins and virtues dead,
      Past the pain from my sordid ways,
Were it not for your angelic past.

Isabella,
I join your heaven, my spirit dazed,
      At peace with you and my forgiving God.

By the Power of Love

With your love, I lay afloat
      the gentle breeze which wafts my face
Beneath your wings, I find refuge
      no pirate asteroid can touch me now,
      no subterfuge can break my will,
An embattled role, I cease to play
      — a victim I cease to be.

You are my haven, my safety net
      from this incongruous universe
      from passion's cacophony
      from the cruel devices of broken men,
I am again reborn
      into a gentle and rejuvenated world,
I need not run —
      I need not hide,
Fear no longer rules my life
      Warped dreams, I do not miss,
          the emotional labyrinth is passe
Renewed and secured by you —
      maligned no longer by the ritual sunset,
Your love permeates my very core
      and scuttles away my autumn twigs.

I need not rummage the past,
No need to re-open ghastly old wounds,
      — re-ignite the searing flames
          the plethora of nightmare
      — of burnt passion,
      — of flesh aggrieved,
Muffling the music of my soul,
      sadly fracturing my dreams.

Today — I feel nothing but infinite joy
      the utmost reverence for life
      — emboldened by your undying love
      — animated by your stars,
I celebrate the demise of pain
      — the effacement of despair,
      — the exodus of perilous dreams,
Rejoicing at the spectacle of light and hope
      made iridescent by your care
Touching rainbow's end —
      exuding glow from the power of your love.

The Final Romance

In awe, I awaken
        to the constellation of the stars,
A tepid cosmos comes alive,
        Gently wafts my soul
in this celestial overplay.

Dancing clouds of resplendent sky
        — the silvery chanting waves
              permeate my spirit,
O' love be a permanence
        in my life.

Unabashed, I cast my lot
        In this enriching covenant,
Perfused in this aroma of delight
        — this joy I have always
              sought and craved.

Mesmerized is my heart
        as peace surrenders —
in this spectral interplay
        of prisms and rainbows
              of sights and sounds
        of mirage and vignettes,
In this magical trance —
In the joy of this *final* romance.

New Romance, Old Romance

I, the dancer of a new romance
        insidiously appear
     optimism parleyed, new landscape drawn,
The tentacles of passion encroach
     — on my teetering resolve
     — on my ambivalence,
Once more, I am mesmerized
     with this illusionary chase.
I am again the clamored prize
     at the doorstep of the vulture's lair,
Grasping at every twig
     and the fallen petals of human warmth.

Vignettes of splintered dreams
     re-appear from my dormant cave:
The hiding place of my private tears
     and fumbled quest,
My soul's history is unraveled
     — the reruns of past romance
Its crack and maze
        looping into a solitary end,
Now a déjà vu for me
     about to be a fallen prey
        to the allures of errant prism.
But the reluctant night arrives
     and its unflinching copious tears,
     — heaven's downpour:
        a prophecy, a cry of doom,
unnerving my placated flesh —
     fizzling my complacency,
Sizzling sky, the lightning strikes
     Its thunderous roar uprooting me,

Reopens the chasm of the past
— unrolling the video of time,
dislocating dreams and rhapsodies
with its tortured ends.

My Soul's Sustenance

I will follow your sun
       drenched in the radiance of your charm,
Your tears of love, like pearls,
       priceless and luminous,
    are my soul's sustenance.

I will dabble in your dreams
    in the life you aspire:
    your pathway to the stars,
       your stars are mine.

When the twilight kisses the night
       — at transition time,
Serenity will permeate
    my flickering spirit,
Pacified I will be
    that I remain forever
       the true love of your life.

Chapter II
Endurance and Attrition

I Know My Place

I weep in the dark
    pressed to make my case
        against the exploiter of souls,
Turning us all into refugees,
    unwilling orphans of the earth,
    unhappy cohorts of society's game.
No plaudits due me,
No empathy from this steely world,
    immersed in its passion,
Steeped in its own way
    its prairie of pain —
    versed in human disconnect,
    digital zeal, genetic tinkering.

Only rejection awaits me —
    Condescending glance
        of the ill-informed,
        from the half-baked,
        from an emotionally labile earth,
            from charred souls.
But, I know my place
    I refuse to peg my life
        with material space
        — these false sanctuaries,
        its shallow entreaties
        its cosmic toppings.

True, we live in a plethora
        of ambiance and dichotomies —
    too many gray zones,
    too many equivocations,
    mixed signals,

disparate cultures, clashing values,
But one fact remains:
Naked we emerge
and naked we will go —
*This is **inescapable**.*

A Straggler for Life

Stifle not my rainbows,
    Siphon not my hopes,
Flecks of sunshine peer through
    my mask,
Permeating the famished atom
    Of my soul,
Inside me — a lost romance,
    Scoffed and scorned,
My amorphous spirit wails,
    One time lucent and incandescent,
        Mystic and nomadic,
            radiant and faithful.

Sonorous voices of the past now
    Echo the starry-eyed lass
        I once was,
Of one who learned to love,
    Lived fully,
Emboldened by the elixir of hope,
    Resonating the lyrics of doom and gloom,
        In the ferris wheel of love,
        Peaking, ebbing,
    of falling stars, of erratic dreams,
Many times broken and revived,
    Wounded and re-scarred,
Somehow I survive,
    A straggler for life.

Why? How?

Why did I stumble?
When did I fail?
Too much feasting
>Too much traffic
>Too many crossroads
>Too many detours

I protested too much
I fought too hard
>For what? For whom?

Why did I falter?
Why was I foiled?
>Was my loss predetermined
>>even before I could
>>>make my case?
>Is fate predestined for all?

Caught in a melee
>of disconnected lives
>>irreverent quests

My reticulated sails
>in a havoc—
>>no escape latch for me,

I shudder in the dark
>*wrinkle in the sunlight.*

Why did I misspeak?
>Who shall I blame?

Groveling in silence—
>I, alone, bear the brunt
>>of my moribund values,
>>>my lonely missteps,

I could have scored better
>appealed more, cajoled less—

But only lethal sounds
        could pour from my tart tongue
   —versed with the venomous
   verbiage of the soul.

And to this very day-
    At winter's end,
I am agaped—wide eyed,
    Perplexed to the end,
Erratic and stupefied—
    I keep asking myself:
        Why? How come?

Neverland

Unglazed, unminted,
    I am in the dockyard of those
        who do not belong,
Too much time, too little room to maneuver—
Confined in the heap of undulating pain,
    in the debris of secular tongs,
    of hip hop and metallic lures,
Sampling the rubbish of tinsel town
    and its skewed heroes,
The media speculate
    in their farcical neons—
While the masses of humanity
    are mesmerized into inaction.
They are denied entry in Neverland
But there is no Neverland—
    Shangrila does not exist
        —only its rubbles.

Thoughts

I am not alone
> but I feel the solitude of the abandoned,

I am not an orphan but I feel like one,
> groping for the human touch.

Survival is no longer economics or spiritual,
> but intellectual.

Life is no longer a tightrope precision,
> it is a constant struggle to keep with the pace.

Life is still enticing,
> but many moments speak of status quo, plateau, and containment.

I feel like the proverbial beast of burden belonging to the legion—
> people who work hard, wake up early, and accomplish very little.

I sleep enough, yet restless is my soul.

But It Hurts As Much

I may not have bruised as hard
    nor hemorrhaged as much,
I was not maimed—
    no dismantled flesh,
No twisted joints
    my mind intact
      with intellect unsullied -
Yet I hurt as much

They did not slice me
    nor uproot me—a new transplant,
      but for me, intrigue is intrigue
    slander is a slander—
And truth is not negotiable.
They could not burn my soul
    erode my ethos
      nor pillage my virtues,
But it hurts as much—
    as if they succeeded.

They could not slash my hopes
    nor blunt my dreams,
They could not still my voice
    nor efface my joy,
A vintage woman, a healer,
    with ardor to serve—
But still, I agonize as much
    with their savagery.

I feel a victim to all
their games of inequities
Like the many preys

      who could not fight back -
      like the flower trampled -
          and the bud stunted,
I am angry that the innocent sunrise
          can be thwarted
              by disingenuous human beings.

I have not mastered
      the art of forgiving—
And I, born in pain—
      reared amidst a war
          which I cannot fathom
cannot let go the unjustness of society
      with its selective values.

It is not easy to forgive,
      to conceal my pain
          and agonize in vain—
when forgiving is not a word
      my foes understand,
It is not the language
      of the predators or perpetrators
          nor those with scuttled values.

I sought my God one day,
      and realized that I am not alone,
His chaste temple now permeates
      my cloistered soul—
More men have been disgraced and denied,
      bloodied and blunted—
As for me, I have learned to forgive,
But still—*it hurts as much.*

Closure

I am past the pain, the hurt, the inebriation
    past the ire, the rancor, the intoxication,
    past rummaging through my eclectic values,
For life is more than just a toxic well gone dry,
    more than just the spiraling of birds—
        to their ethereal plane,
    not merely the unmasking of men's dark side
        his satanic claim,
It is also a revelation of men's goodness and greatness,
        the just jubilation to the eternal spring.

I am past dodging the waves to self-inflict,
    past the savage quest to unseat—
        vulgar men and their worthless needs.
I am past the ferocious jaws of disgrace.
    past the threatening carnal vibes,
    past the mirage which choked each dream,
    past land mines, quicksand which sucks me in
        —to my beaten path,
        where I strayed—my fun-filled years,
        where naive virtues embraced the thorn,
        —entangled in its chaotic forms.

I am past the dreary tunnel of the track
    —the hidden caves of endless wait—unrequited love,
    hard work unrewarded, loyalty uncompensated
    justice in abeyance, hope unanswered,
past the dying inferno of unbridled passion,
past the chasm from endless nights,
past the claws of the human flesh—
    of honor lost,
past the fire, the goal, the dream,

in vain searching for one just man,
awaiting His verdict,
    His judgment near,
awaiting His mercy,
    my cross to bear.

Chapter III
Bonding

He Will Be Back
-My Son

He might bid farewell
    But like Joseph given up for dead
        —he will be back again in triumphant march
        —dispensing warmth and love,
            forgiveness to his detractors
                —a new beginning.

He might leave—but just for a while
    He might spurn the twigs of yesterday
        but mark my word, he will be back
        —to return to the ashes of his nascency
        —to retrieve the castaway bloom
            and replant the seeds: his epiphany.

He might weep
    But he will recover and be back in control
        —his precious tears to soften
        the unyielding shell
            and glaze its rough edges.

Gone for awhile—away from his nest
    Past many winters
        while helpless and hopeless
            loved ones wait,
He will be back—
    This seed of mine
Our branch, our bud
    This bloom—my son.

He at 80

Somewhat frayed,
  His spine gently bent,
    in a decorous stoop
      of one who once carved
        a romantic pose—
that muscular genome
      he once displayed.

He reads his mail,
His double-rimmed glasses—
    more like a pathologist
      with his microscope,
      peering intently at
      each letter—bills and invitations
as if encrypted.

From my vantage view,
    with half the light allowed
      from incandescent bulbs
      replaced by mini-voltage
        for austerity—
Streaks of silver emerge
  from his dormant top
    and receding space of his brow,
Vainly trying to imply—
    He once had flair
      in his own time and space—
      and I cannot help but shed
      copious tears of deep longing.

My Papa Would Be Mighty Proud

If my father was alive today
    he would help me parry the thrust
  From the extraneous waves
    which errantly bruised my heart,
      intruding into my pristine soul—
  before I learned to dive,
    before I learned to trust,
  before I could refuel
    my tank of faith.
If my father was alive today
  He would cast a lending hand
    as I wriggle from my cocoon,
    to be freed from the spider web,
  He would untie the knot that
    has clipped my nascent wings
      —before I learned to glide
      before I learned to sing and dance.
If my father was alive today
  He would swell with pride
    that I "done him some good,"
    that I chose to walk
      on molten ground—
      on snake-infested swamps
And willingly carried the cross—
  absorbed the thorns
    with my bloodied palms
  because it is the right thing to do
Because I'd rather bleed and agonize
  than indulge in the slimy values
    of an errant world.
Indeed, if my papa was alive today—
  He would be mighty proud!

The Awaited

A bulb syringe, a warmer,
    a stethoscope, a thermometer,
A pushcart, an incubator,
    an oxygen tank-lifelines for
        the coming creation,
Trust not the sorcerers,
    not the quacks,
Trust not the politicians,
    the rabble rousers—
The *coming one* is real:
      all flesh and bone,
    —the bloom before the petals
    —the dew before the teardrops,
      the sprout before the beanstalk,
The heir apparent to a humanity,
Sadly, corrupted and repudiated.

Forget that love didn't play
    a relevant role
Forget that the bearer of the sperm
      is in denial—
  that the carrier womb
    is not ready or worthy,
Forget that the liaison
      is not anointed,
    that it was "just an accident"—just a fling,
    —that it was sporadic and nomadic,
      tenuous and strained,
Ignore the dissipated romance
    the disrupted lives,
    the unredeemed trust,
Ignore the unpaid bills,

overdue charge accounts,
Earth knows no greater fury
    than the wrath of a physician
    with unpaid bills of her own!

Forget that the world is teeming
    with wolves and jaguars,
    that it is a dumping ground.
    of jackals and foxes
that the poor lamb had no chance.

Today, we welcome
    this marvelous creation—
    reeling us in our doomsday
    approach to life,
This very hour—*sunshine emerges*,
We glimpse, we grasp
    the bud before it sprouts,
We touch the new roots, the infantile branches,
    away from the discarded twigs
    of disgraced lives,
The new migrant, this tender one is here—
    unscathed and pure!
A renewed citizenry is in the offing,
    past a faltering humanity,
    past a human race
    who has surrendered and succumbed,
At this very moment, there is hope!

Alma

I heave and sigh,
    brood and retreat,
But the dogs need
    their kennels cleaned—
The cows need to be milked
    the goats need to graze.

The faucet leaks,
    the floor needs mopping,
Last night, the wind blew off
    the slate from our concrete roof
        —just like that,
Just like the night
    my friend's life was snuffed out.

She was swept by the west wind
    rambling through our eerie nights,
It rankled life's relevance—
    even as we held onto hope,
She could have been swept
      by the East wind,
    but long ago she left
        the eastern shores for her
            new found land.
What does it matter now?

One day a farmer lost his wife,
    he ached and mourned,
Sunrise and sunset
    fused into amorphous veil,
His wound deeply etched,
    bleeding and weeping

but the fields need to be plowed
        the seeds sown.
Soon it will be harvest time,
the wheat needs to be threshed
      —just like the rice
            in her native land.

And so we go on
         through the motions,
Bereaved ones, loved ones—
     moving, not mourning
No longer groaning—
     as we do each day's task
         in the mechanics of life.
One day,
     He will summon us
to the grandstand—
Each of us in our time,
     in our space,
But we should be ready
     for Alma,
         my dearest friend
     this woman of elegance,
        of angelic grace
     has come and shown the way.

My Papa's Canoe and Me

My papa gave me a canoe,
    one day I fell overboard
        but managed to hang on,
I survived the fall,
    set back the canoe and surged on,
I did not allow the contemptuous side of earth
    to deter me
    —to side sweep my focus
        to stymie my resolve,
I held on — parried the onslaught
    of occlusive forces,
        fended off the attacks of my foes,
            their poisonous fangs
Simply because they thought
    they were the "chosen race."

In my heart, I know my Papa would approve,
    His canoe in me will sail on forever.

Latino Is In

Past my prime — 42 years
    in my adoptive land—
No longer an underdog
    but still understated,
Past civil rights, women rights,
    animal rights, affirmative action—
        I need to re-tool myself.
True, I mastered the Yankee's nasal twang,
    adept with the Southern drawl,
    and the Western cowboy's "bring it on"
        or "make my day" complex,
It took me years
    to "perfect" my act
But I now face a new reality:
    Latino is in!

Years ago, I was not Anglo enough
    (and never will be for that matter!)
Passed up for promotion, isolated—
    ignored by a society unprepared for my kind,
Toastmaster, garden club, square dancing
    helped some
I worked so hard to belong—to be accepted
    I finally could communicate!
Today at 66—now a vintage woman,
    Latino is in and I can't speak the language
    but at least I have the accent
        with Malayan undertones.
But what will I do now?
It took me so long to learn
    the Yankee lingo.
I can't just ignore

      my Anglo friends
I truly enjoy them
      for who they are.

I am not ready to morph
      to be fitted with another mask and wig,
Am not ready for another re-tooling or re-inventing,
My generic days are over
      I can't adapt—I can't adjust
         a trial balloon, a loner,
            a maverick forever.
O' cruel age, O' cruel times
      I never could make it right.
Anglo was then—
      Latino is now.

I Chose America

I saluted another flag
    sailed another ocean
    chose another sunset
    listened to my own clarion,
    festooned my own rainbow.

I quelled my inner longings,
    even my longings for the
        land of my birth,
I fought another battle,
    another nation's war,
    alongside my newly
        ordained brothers.

I defended my adoptive land,
    against those who assaulted
        its institutions,
    against those who terrorized
        its soul,
    against those who preyed
        on its weakness -
    attempting to dislodge its core,
        usurp its goodness.

'Tis not the rejection of my ancestors,
    not the disavowal of my culture and race,
    nor betrayal of my island paradise
      the country of my birth,
Rather, it is giving back
    to my America of four decades
    what it has given me:
    freedom, opportunities,

and the ability to coexist in peace—
to resurge, to renew -
to be pivotal in this nation of laws—
to partake in its growth and greatness.

In the end— a country is my country
    when it opens its vistas,
A home is my home
    where I am nurtured and welcomed,
And for those who believed in America
    who have benefited by its generosity -
    who worked hard and bore the yoke of uncertainty,
I say: be a pillar, be a comet,
    become a torch bearer for freedom,
        for humanity,
rectify the iniquities
be a torch for peace—
As for me — I chose America.

Our Son Is Back
-It Is Harvest Time

Enhancer of our stage,
Enhancer of our needs,
   Our son is back—
He now returns to the primacy of his nest,
    Bubbling and leaping
       to the warmth of his abode,
The visceral youth is back
    twirling with maturity.

Like a plant stunted—
      In time our child has unfurled his petals
         of filial love-
    into our craving and waiting soul—
    Unleashing our parental passion
        —once a tortured path,
His dissident wings rejuvenated
      with its tonic glide —
    flapping gently, its frayed edges
       —a poignant testimony to his many falls.
Bruises and scratches now healed
      from a naive college child
         —confounded by dichotomies.
He has finally found his niche,
    his identity cleared,
  Proud of his chiseled look
        —at ease with his cultural milieu,
  No apologies to make.

We, his parents, are no longer
        "strange" or "queer"

And I, his mother,
        am no longer "nutty" or "odd."
So what if we are not fashionable
    with our multicolored braids
        —living multi-phasic lives,

His countenance clearly speaks of
    his pride and esteem—
        his fondness and affection
           of the roots he comes from,
At *long last* we are now relevant,
    standing tall at all times—
And my son simply knows
    as he blooms and ripens—
That it is <u>now</u> our
Harvest Time.

Chapter IV
Wisdom and Transition

Life's Performance

We form alliances, then we regroup,
    We dispense forgiveness and ask for mercy ourselves,
We fine-tune our thoughts to realign the mechanics of life,
    We overhaul our engine and recharge our battery,
We strengthen our physique and master our emotions,
    We keep groping for the right words and adapting a
    different stance,
We follow the abc's of our earlier nurturing—
    even as we tinker, modify, and recreate it.

At times we have done better than our forbears—
    a few times we far outpaced them.
Many times just to be at par with our elders or our peers
would suffice,
    A few times we seem never to get it, never to win it.
Sometimes the prize seems to be within our grasp:
    the promised land is at hand.
We climb and clamber only to fall, and without hesitation we
try again,
    only to come out with the same results.
By sheer persistence, we are able to negotiate ourselves out
of a quandary—
    escape the bruising quagmire,
but Oh! so much trauma, so much fracture,
    and the permanent concussion of our souls.

Without our engine being rechecked or our wheels being
aligned,
    we are apt to go back—
Again and again through the same ruinous path and the same
old results.

Unless we allow ourselves to be greased by the oil of the basics
    and allow the spirit to take over,
Unless we allow the angels to navigate us through the deep waters—
    shedding off the chemical and emotional abuse—
We won't be able to run the engine of life
    and keep our motor running.

I Got In
(A Case for Affirmative Action)

I have tripped and fallen,
>   pushed and pulled—
>>   retreated in solace—
>   poised to revive my ardor,
>>   regain my strength—
>>>   but to no avail,
>   *simple determination*
>>   *was not enough.*

I dived in the murk,
>>   swam torrential seas,
>   turmoil didn't unravel me,
>   my enemies did not faze me—

Persistence didn't get me in,
>   — I was shut out from the system
>   ... a veritable outsider.

I reasoned and cajoled,
>   Fumed and pleaded
>>   *but I could not*
>>>   *penetrate the barrier,*

Honesty didn't matter,
>   hard work unrewarded,

Sacrifice taken for granted
>   good intentions ignored.
>>   quality work didn't count.

One night, I dreamt I was an American
>   —and I awoke as one,

Hastily, I put on my suit,
>   went to the courthouse,

    filed my briefs—
    slammed a million-dollar suit
        against my perpetrators:
            those who stymied my chances,
                derailed my drehis band of ma-
                levolent men,
        steeped in their own xenophobia,
I charged them with outright racism
and discrimination —
And this time, I got in.

Forgiving the Enemy

Across the boardroom is my foe:
    vile, wicked, ugly,
He is contemptuous and despicable
    a cross to bear
He treks alone — joyless,
    escapes through the revolving door
        of freedom,
How he gets away
    with his skewed ways
I do not know —
He responds to a different siren
    Listens to his own sound bites,
His manners are caustic —
    his values stunted,
He is anathema to all good people
We are opposite in every sense —
    no reason to connect, to intersect
        no redeeming features —
Chiasmic our souls
    the only common thread;
We both belong to the human race
    with bare knuckles and crimson blood
        flowing through our veins,
And the only nexus is God telling us:
We are all part of His flock
        and that somehow
        —we must try to forgive.

America Is Not for All

Why did they think life is good
    —America is not for all,
The bastion of freedom-loving men
        who want to make a go of life
    Past racial and social barricades
    Past the bruising detours —
        into the verdant fields
        of opportunities.
America remains the Utopia of immigrants
    —the Shangri-La for those willing
        to take the gauntlet
    —for those willing to plant and replant,
    where persistence is still the name of the game.

But America is not for the bleeding heart
    —not for the meek, the tender or the naive,
    not for the teetering or the wishy washy,
    —not for the imperfect, the quiet, the old,
        the impaired or the unhealthy
        the onion-skinned or the petrified soul,
It is a double-edged sword — a dichotomy,
    A Paradise to many,
    — a Hell to some.

A Transplant

A plant rooted in another soil
        from another wilderness
      cannot simply carry its weight
        and waltz with ease into
           its new abode,
One cannot readily rip its anchor
        from its encased womb—
    to be transformed overnight
        as a "well-adjusted immigrant"
        or the so-called New American.

Like men, a plant needs time
    to sense its space—
    to warm to another lullaby,
        to savor another wine,
Like men, it takes time
    to define its color—
    imbue ardor,
    realign its roots,
    imbibe new nutrients
        —accept new impositions.

Each new migration
        every move—
    calls for another card,
      another scheme
          another stroke,
New ethos comes to play
    new ethics, too,
Clashing with our inbred
    chords and concepts,
Loneliness augments

        the pain of adjustments,
        the chattering of cymbals
        of mixed cultures
                and dissonant mores,
Like men, the plant brings
            its own aroma—
spicy, redolent, awesome—
yet to some-pungent and sour,

Old habits die hard—
    lives often fumbled,
New philosophies emerge,
    traditions morphed,
            meanings parsed,
A new branch, a new baby
    needs to find its own way—
    to grow, to blend, to be pliant,
    awash with mixtures of history—
    of heritage, exciting and dramatic.
Until the "graft" take—

    the new transplant must bear the toll,
            from the trauma of migration—
                until it will finally belong—
But until then,
    it remains an intruder to many,
            an alien an outsider, a carpetbagger—
Such is the fate of the transplant.

Mea Culp
- from an immigrant's child

I rejected my mother's milk
    I discounted her views,
        I was annoyed by her nuances,
I dismissed her creed
        — made light of her culture,
            derided her counsel.

My parents' ways were
    outside my comfort zone
    — annoying and embarrassing,
    old fashioned, irrelevant,
    alien to my social landscape
    — outside the spectrum
        where I evolved.

An immigrant's pride and hope
    as the child of a transplant,
I was perplexed by the racial divide
    and the cultural milieu,
        which gnawed my self-esteem
            and-blurred my view,
I parried this dichotomy with ineptitude,
    I snapped with seething rage —
Awkward to my parents' show of affection,
    protesting their intrusiveness,
Yet, I expected their largesse
    with no qualm,
I accepted their support
    with nonchalance.

I maligned their accent,
    I scorned their culture,
Their interests were far flung'
from mine,
My ways were businesslike,
my style — blunt,

To them I was cold and detached,
    curt and insensitive,
        selfish and self-serving,
I dismissed their yearnings —
    ignored their dreams,
    their ethnicity, their history.

I was their vesper, their high note,
    their essence,
I fueled their grit,
    fueled their spirit
I was their sustenance
    through grinding hours, grueling days,
I was their hope for
    a viable tomorrow.

But all children eventually
    grow up,
A teenager, Yankee or not,
    does not stay a teen forever,
The higher the illusionary podium
    the more abrupt is the fall,
The grander the pedestal,
    the more painful the downward slide,
The cacophony of hormonal disarray receded,
    transformed is the child into a sedate human being,
    gone is the cocky teenager

Now chastened, now civil
  — no longer subject to peer pressure
    nor attracted to false fragrance,
    or beholden to creamy toppings,
Chastened by mistakes I have learned
  the language of civility.
Today, I am where
  I should be,
My parents' travails have become
  my battle cry,
  my footing, my covenant,
They are pearls of endurance —
  their terms of endearment,
They are my elixir of life.

No Such Thing as Charred Hope

Giddy, I spin in thought
    of heaven misspent,
Like a marooned sailor
    in the sea of nowhere,
Like a ship skidding side to side,
    hoisted and thrusted against
        the frigid water of fate
        in the stormy waters of life,
Like a lost hunter in the sunless jungle
    unable to forge a pathway out -
But there is no such thing
    as perpetual despair
    or a permanent abyss -
We rise and fall, ebb and peak,
We hurt, we heal, and rebuild,
Pain and relief interlock,
    despair and reprieve intertwine,
This is the human story.
But as long as the spirit prevails
    regardless of battles won and lost
We will have rebirths and epiphanies,
There is no such thing as a nullified life,
    or a thousand deaths,
No such thing as charred hope
    no such thing as a lost heaven.

From Both Sides Now

We are all borrowers and lenders,
    Perpetrators or victims—
        in certain ways, in many forms
We keep our tongues in check—
    afraid to expose our runaway passions
        and reveal our ugly side.
We are preachers and listeners—
We expound and discourse
    listen selectively—
    in denial or self-preservation
But man is not deaf or dumb forever —
He could capture the mike and own the podium.

Oh — a lifetime of walking the tight ropes—
    Of being precise while teetering on the edge,
    —adjusting to our turbines or that of others,
    skirting past missteps for future serenity,
We call that Karma where I come from.

We cannot always double talk nor do double turns —
    That's for the politicians to do.
We cannot nix life just because we
    —picked the wrong color
    —dug the wrong hole
    —and drilled in the wrong spot.

One day we won't be able to re-invent the wheel,
    nor pivot from the opposite lane -
Chastened, we still can recover but when twilight demands
    more tempo than our choppy emotion can give —
We might not resurge.

We then need to redefine the meaning of failure and
 success—
only to embrace the vestigial joy because that is life
 —no matter what.

Sunshine is my Ally

I would no longer rivet with pleasure,
    my riverbed, arid,
        depleted, my water of life,
A doomed falls has ceased its flow —
    sealing my reservoir,
My ordeal has just begun.

At times, I have been in the wrong lane,
    reversing my course when jolted,
In and out, I skated
    in the inescapable passion of life.
Short-lived is my pain
    and shorter-lived my joy —
        fleeting, teetering, vanishing.

Pearls of laughter gone
    from my impish lips,
But patches and scraps of light remain
Imperiled my spurious music,
    one time scintillating,
But desolation is not my goal,
    despair, not my creed,
Sunshine is my ally —
    to derail the advances of my foes:
        these rooters of destruction
Innocence must be reclaimed.

Today, I am ready to ward off
    the adversarial ploy —
        permeate the shell of redemption.
I am prepared to weld
    the cogent past to the relevant present,

        —without fanfare,
I welcome the alliance
    of the stars and waiting angels,
I am ready to re-join
    the great interplay of rain and sunshine,
        of souls in need —
            its obeisance to Heaven.

Chapter V
Wonderment and Hope

Let the Day Begin: Life's Amalgam

Let the day begin with the rivers and oceans of wonder,
    Let the day begin with fallen leaves
        reattached to their stem—
        like homeless children reunited with their parents,
    Let the day begin with the roar of a moral earthquake
        crushing men's malevolence—
        effacing the malice which has seeped his soul,
    Let the day begin with peaks and valleys,
        cracks and fissures of humanity
leveled into a plane of tolerance and temperance,
    Let the day begin with angelic meteors
        colliding and rambling through this maelstrom of life.
Let the day begin preparing for the night
    when tiny little stars band together
        to outshine and outlast the brazen sun,
Let the day begin with the untouchable coming down to earth
    and the unfathomable brought to simplicity,
Let the day begin with the righteous man
    prevailing against a tepid world,
Let the day begin conjuring splendor
    from the mud and hut of rickety lives—
Let the day begin with fallen angels
    dethroned from space—
        His anger assuaged.

Let the day end—
    in His wonder and justice,
    in His kindness and mercy,
For only then is the cycle of life complete—
    the beginning and end of life is one,

day and night fused,
the soul and body synergized,
"Dust thou art to dust returnest"
is truly spoken from the soul.

Born Free

Born wild, born free—
    In the jungle mall,
        in my island paradise,
Rocking in my sleep
      —dancing with the leaves,
Unwilling to be muted
      —to be clamped
        —to be transplanted.
I cast my stake from the forest glades
    in my quest for freedom,
      to be left alone in my flight, in my solitude
Unwilling to submit my destiny
      to the social ghettos
        of this plastic world—
          their flaws and constrictive chains,
Better to Join the dust and ashes of fate
  —wallow in the elements of the earth,
  be a solitary speck
  just to be free again.

Not the Meekest Lamb

I may not be the meekest lamb
    or the most pliant pet—
   But I carry with me the longevity
    of wisdom of years,
I may not be a penthouse
    harboring the magnificent view
       or salivating in the comfort of the rich—
   But I harbor prudence
    knowing my priority — focused on my goals,
At times I may be accused of temerity
But mistake it not for impetuousness
    for I do not carry the harshness of the
       proud,
Even the Son of God humbly knelt
    to wash men's feet,
    — was crucified so men might live
      and know His might
   Clearly He has set the tone for me—
Bold or meek as you may perceive me to be
   I have made the best of choices:
    A lust for peace
    A life of love
    Simply, I am proud to be His.

Am Ready for the Bloom

At the sound of spring
    and its cherished vibes,
The root awakens
    from its ritual sleep,
The skeletal twig
    parades its embryonic bud—
Soon to unfurl
    its long-awaited bloom,
Ready to retake the world
    with its spiraling joy,
Once more, I await a new beginning
    another chance to play—
    revel in my own repertoire—
        Perhaps my last?

Never Too Late for a New Bud

A life snuffed
A bloom rebuffed,
    limpid petals, vanishing fragrance,
You have stymied my every move
    slashed my dreams -
    intruded in my pristine life
    —leaving me alone to sulk,
    condemned in my fragile shell.

My petals forced to weep
    —warped before their time,
Yet past this stage
Above the mercurial fray
    it is not too late
        for the emergence of a new bud
The renaissance of my tepid soul
    the noble blossoming of my heart.

Always the Spirit Flows

Be good to me
    for I will not always be here for you.
Fate has its own perfidious moods
    like the tropics has its monsoons.
Nothing in life is certain —
    even the logical does not follow.

Nothing is truly predictable
    even the rational.
In a moment, I can be drawn by the West wind
    never to return—
Sucked by the quicksand of life
    into an impenetrable clutch
    never to resurface.

In a moment, the murky water of life and it pollutants
    can choke me in to oblivion.
At any time, each of us has
    a sward of Damocles to fear,
    an awaiting flood,
    an earthquake lurking —
crumbling and cracking our very foundation

In a moment life can be snuffed out
    like a petal
    like feather plucked
    like dust blown and displaced
But life is not only inane
nor insane.

It is a dichotomy I present to you —
    not to be fatalistic,
But to be contemplative,
    not to be hopeless,
But to be open for adversity.
To allow the spirit to take hold,
    to sprout its buds,
    spread its wings.

Men come and go
I might be gone for you —
    but *always* The Spirit flows.

Spring, Autumn, Sunset

In the spring of our lives
    we play and flirt
    dive and dunk
        as ducklings do
    — in this dawn of our infancy.
For it takes time to find ourselves
    to define our role, our special niche
        in the planetary space
If we gracefully injure our wings
    while pecking each others grain
    we can easily forgive and excuse
        each other's oddities
    the greasy seasoning of our
        blooming year.

But when our roots take hold
    and our branches grow
        in the early autumn of our lives-
We should know by then our vulnerabilities
        — the limitation of our stars,
    Hate and doubt should leave no marks
    — Intemperance resolved
Darkness ferreted out
        — and all the hugging and haggling,
        cussing and fuming should be passe.
    Warmth and gentleness triumphant.

At the sunset of our voyage
        in this wild existence
    The past may sometimes resurface
        regrets and remorse recycled —
        pain revived

But we need not beat ourselves
    with the rubbles of the past
No need to rummage through elusive dreams,
    the unfilled expectations of the past
Time is too precious at this dimming twilight
    all shadows must be quelled
        as another generation arrives.

Let the gleaming light
    of our peace prevail
Let us pave the road for our grandchildren
    the newest petals of mutation
For they need to go through the same
        cycle of life
    To slip, to bloom, to peck, to glide,
Hopefully injuring loss their wings
    and maintaining longer
        their ecstatic scent.

This Is My Moment

This is my moment
    I have unearthed my soul,
Subverted my foes,
    no angst or trepidation,
    no hidden emotions,
        no slit in my resolve,
My passion unsullied
    — innocence must not be shredded.

I repelled the bullies of life,
    I repulsed their waves of untruth,
        on serrated pathways,
    on cavernous byways,
I exposed their devious schemes:
    to frame raw minds with
        their sham philosophies —
    to instill their convoluted mores.

Let them clash with the luckless vipers,
    let them vilify each other,
Let the grapes of scorn
    self-destruct and demolish
        their wooden souls,
The earth is brighter without
    their feckless vision,
The earth is better off
    without their divisive presence.
Indeed — this is my moment.

Beyond the desperate foray
    of despicable men,
Looms the sky, the stars, the sun, and meadows

    riveting with the grandiose roses
        and daffodils of life,
    eclipsing all that is unworthy of the earth,
Now — past life's tsunamis —
I emerge secure of my role,
    secure in my faith,
Indeed, this is my moment.

Life Is Beautiful

There is music in the air—
    There is music everywhere,
When I reach the peak of love and meet the
    dawn of life,
There is feasting in the field,
    There is gaiety everywhere
When my fledging soul is fused with
Heaven's incantation
    —the perpetual rites of God,
There is unspeakable awe to the overdue symphony—
    the music splashing its hypnotic spell
        to a teetering humanity,
    converting despondency into Divine melody,

No more unjustified trust—
    faith at last vindicated, hope reaffirmed—
    the maternal fire once more on the roll,
    believing in each grain of sand
        that a child brings home.

Each pebble dotting the pristine sand
    glistens with the sunlight of history,
Each fallen seed from each tiny grain
    will bear again a starting plant.
The maternal voyage is on again—
    leaving not an iota of doubt
mother—a child is back on the course,
God's gentle intrusion is evident—
Eternal celebration is at hand,
Earth is illuminated by flames so dazzling—
    as they outdo the icons of mistaken lives.
Finally—music is back in the air,

There is music beyond compare
    —with the Eternal Conductor.
Indeed, life is beautiful.

CPSIA information can be obtained
at www.ICGtesting.com
Printed in the USA
JSHW020342300622
27500JS00001B/2

Dr. Simeon S. Mayuga
5306 W. Irving St.
Pasco, WA 99301-3004